Prelude....

Brought on by innocence lost and knowledge gained,

Learned all the ways I've been betrayed,

Tried for peace but the effort was lost

Now vengeance won't quench what the fury begot...

Madness

A Touch of Madness

A touch of madness,

An insatiable thirst,

To hold in the palm of your hand

All the beauty of the universe

Within the lover's eye,

In the depth of the poet's soul,

A fool's courage resides

And stands betwixt the earth and the next

Beyond a longing for freedom,

And desire for defeat,

The knowledge that the purest regard

Lies betwixt honesty and deceit

Fairytale

Upon entering this foreign land are some things you must understand

Saints and sinners oft walk hand in hand

With the beasts only the meek persevere...

For only the most humble ask for what they deserve

It's alright just turn off your eyes and smile

It's been dead here for a while

Of the children not much is known

One with the mind of a sinner and one with a mind of her own

Spawn of the honest and the deceitful

Born running from all of the world's evil

Stone cold honesty sleeps with a shield built at a young age

To save herself from the deranged

Still detached from what she feels

You may not see her but she's real

Why don't you turn off your eyes and smile?

It's been dead here for a while

With all the warmth of her lies and the secrets inside

She can't undo what she has made

A child that doesn't know her name

An endless wanderer to this day

She was delivered with anguish and pain....

Given no pennies for happiness she has made

It's been dead here for a while,

Now turn off your eyes and smile,

While your lips are eternally shut with a bloody nail,

Welcome to my fairytale

Sunset Eyes

Sunset eyes and upside-down smile

Half her mind closed, her will is dying

And still she is asking,

"Now what can the world be hiding?"

To be happy you must sever

All ties with those who hurt you

And ruin their lives

You keep on betraying and forgiving

What is the point of this kind of living?

There is a hole in your heart where you carry their pain

It is only yourself that you can blame

Decadent sorrow painted with smiles

Thoughts continue to fill with bile…

Fragments of anguish in a

Body not your own

Timeless traveler searching for a home

Decay of flesh, illusion of escape

Self-destruct, but not as an act of hate

Decadent sorrow washes away

As you learn the importance of today...

A lesson is learned a little too late

And one sunset eye with symptoms of death

Awaits her one final breath...

The Kingdom of Heaven

Decay of innocence

Abolition of moral

You started it

Invited me inside

I've caught every thought

That slipped your mind

I've kept them with me

Only to be borrowed, my dear

For the occasion you wizen up

And long for the soul of yesteryear

Once naivety is lost

And cynicism taken its place

With a heart turned to stone

You'll realize your mistake

Do not fret, my dear

I've held onto your innocence

As well as your fears

To reach out you must open your heart,

For the kingdom of heaven was yours from the start

Detained

I'm sick of my senses

They leave me defenseless

Leave me detained,

Confined and restrained

In this mortal vessel

My face for today

I'm sick of my senses

They leave me defenseless

From this onslaught

Of chaos and commotion

Of uncontained emotion

I'm a slave to the shadows

Isolation my only reset

Empathy a gift and curse

It makes me kind

Then drains my soul

And I'm cold and alone

I'm sick of my senses

They leave me defenseless

Leave me detained

Confined and restrained

In this mortal vessel

My face for today

The Bells

Harken to the bells

And to the ticking clock

Harken to the bells

May the incessant dinging never stop

Harken to the bells

And the ringing inside your head

Harken, harken

Have you heard a word I've said?

Harken to the bells

And the wisdom they bestow

The time has come for your sins

The others need to know

Harken to the bells

The thunderous cries

Harken to crestfallen tears

And ask yourself why

Harken to the bells

And to the ticking clock

Harken to the bells

Because once they cease, you'll stop

Years Gone By

As I pass along the graves

Ruminating past my days

Where is the wind? Where is the sun?

A breath, a shiver, from someone?

Dust and roses, heart ablaze

I caught a tear, or was that rain?

Voices distant, muted, an echo

My roots are deep, ne'er to let go

He used to visit day by day

Years gone by, come what may

Bereft am I of hands entwined,

Beyond all thought of space and time

He used to visit day by day

Years gone by, yet I remain

Do Not Mourn

Why so lost? Why so glum?

You've every possibility under the rising sun

The moon, the stars, to be taken by any means

As long as you shake your head and awake from your dreams

Heed my words and

Listen to me

Do not mourn dear, for yesterday

Do not cry over knowledge gained

'Twas easier to be free

When you were young and naïve

Heed my words and

Listen to me

Do not mourn the child you were yesterday

For you can still be free

Come down from the ivory tower

Do not recoil from embrace

Reclaim your power

Freedom is yours to taste

It is your choice, but not your right,

No use holding back, contrite

You traded innocence for wisdom

And only you can break free from your prison

Retribution

I've bloodied my hands

Got dirt in my soul

It's the same story again

And it's growing old

If I find retribution

Then atone for my crimes

Who'll suffer for penance

For actions that were mine

I can't give up

But I must give in

I don't have the strength

But I've got the will

Even the heart of a sinner

Who has been wronged

Can learn to forgive

And learn to move on

Fallen

I've been told the end is nigh

I say it's already beginning

Lucifer insidiously gaining power

And I think that he is winning

For now everything has a shelf life

Vanity has beaten unity

Innocence is a sin and

Wisdom is forsaken for beauty

Though God only looks inside

Longing for ascension

I've been stripped of my wings

I've joined the ranks of the fallen

And every tear stings

The Myth and Memory

You shan't speak ill of the passed,

The downtrodden or the deranged-

So what is there left to say?

I've been sweet and

I've been sour

Taken for a goddess

Then called a liar

Trapped within the dream

And the desire

I'll become more myth than memory

A fable crafted by thine lips

If that is as you wish it

I shall cease to exist

I know I should be grateful

I know I should be glad

But my grip is tenuous

And my work is all I've had

And all that is left of the memory and the myth

Is a transient fantasy

Though all I had wanted

Was for someone to think of me

A sweet comedy

I lie betwixt

A myth and a memory

That won't be missed

Graceless

Happy to be nameless, invisible, forgettable

But to lose my own heart is nothing but regrettable,

A quest for beauty, respect, prosperity,

When all I long for is soul bound serenity

Seduced by the serpent

For the fruit I yearned

Now I wish I could repress what I have learned

I've grace in my movement

Glide along the floor

But grace in my soul

There is no more

There is no more

Fallen into a world not my own

I built an ivory tower where I stay, alone

For protection the walls so strong and high

And I can't get out even if I try

Immortality

This breath was meant to be the last

So I don't have to deal with my past

Grievances and sorrows

Fleeing the thought of tomorrow

This breath was meant to be the last

But I can't catch a break

Was this a mistake?

The draw of serenity within a dreamless sleep

Was but a lie within a dream

A swallow of air begets surprise

And I start to open up my eyes

Suddenly my body is mine no more

Feeling lost and unsure

My lack of vocabulary

Is both humbling and scary,

Speech is futile so I cry,

With a warm embrace my tears are dry

This breath was meant to be the last

But I will not forsake my second chance

Outcast

Outcasts,

They exist within a mask,

They hold their hearts,

They hold their tongues,

But they have eyes and ears;

Pensive, wise beyond their years

(But no one there to catch their tears)

Purgatory

It starts with weakening of the resolve

It starts with a waterfall

I no longer have access to my logical brain

And my only excuse is I've gone insane

It starts with anger

It starts with a flame

I wish I had somebody to blame

Life's not fair and it never was

I guess someone's provoking with us from above

It starts with a quickening of the pulse

It starts with a puzzle I just can't solve

Try as I may and as I might

I just really don't want to fight

It ends with acceptance

It ends with defeat

The end of the rainbow I'll never see

This will be my eternity

I guess I'll just have to learn to like purgatory

Painted Face

Once life was effortless

And I was carefree

I was on top of the world

And the world bowed down to me

I never stopped moving

I never said please

With the wink of an eye

You'd be weak in the knees

But all I have are pretty words

And a painted face

And I'm drowning in this barrenness

That I'm destined to embrace

I could remove the mask

And wear my true face

But I've never had to ask

All I can do is take

If I ask for council

And heed your advice

At the cost of my pride

Perhaps I could learn to play nice

The Riddle

It started with a puzzle

Then ended with a riddle

Through the smoke and debris

Still, I'm caught in the middle

Of the earth and stars,

Venus and Mars

My grip is slipping from your open arms

It started with a puzzle

That would never be complete

I thought I had all the pieces

But they turned to dust

And returned to the sea

And I'm ever-unknowing

And yearning for more

I've come to embrace the riddle,

Ever-unsure-

For why settle for certainty

Before you've reached the shore?

The Illusionist

Rain drops falling from the ground

Turn the world upside down

Right or wrong, black or white

You'll see what I want

And you won't fight

I'll spin you a web of deepest desire

So soak it all in, flying higher and higher

Evade my mischief, trickery, deceit

Persuade yourself not to believe what you see

Is it magic or a trick of the mind?

There is no time to run or hide

Still the mirage will persist

I'm no wizard, just the illusionist

Turn to stone

A gentle heart

A steadfast gaze

Can only last until it breaks

Deceitful and malicious souls

Feast upon flesh and bone

The smallest light overcomes the dark

And a curse is placed upon my heart

Close my eyes cover my ears

The time, at last, is near

For now I see, but all I know

Is that I want to go home

Only time can tell

If I'll ever break the spell

This slave is free of chains

And will rebel again

But vengeance is for the weak

Lord, tame my tongue not to speak

I'll prove forgiveness is an art

Though all that will remain is me and my stone heart

Angel of Death

Hidden beneath a body of lies

Hardened eyes keep secrets inside

Brushes with innocence

Tears fall from their eyes

White lies White lies

Inside he dies (dies)

Cracked wings result in crooked flight,

Taking one down to hell tonight,

Non- attachment, detachment

Balance hard to keep,

Children ripped from their bodies in their sleep

This isn't what he does to you

It's what he does to himself

Stealing souls from perceived mortal wealth

With each fire extinguished,

With each heart that breaks

Everything he does feels like a mistake

Angel of Death

Saves the world from the living

Appears to take without giving

Angel of Death

Harden your heart

Otherwise you might just fall apart

The Voice

There is a voice deep inside

I've heard it before, I know it's mine

Smiled through destruction of inner walls

In my veins as the blood falls

There is a voice deep inside

And it's taking over my mind

Cobwebs caught all my lost thought

Dazed throughout this battle I lost

There is a voice, there is a voice

And it won't stop...

Vanity

Inside the haunted palace, my earthbound home

The souls who live there feel all alone

Piece by piece, part by part,

One by one they're falling apart

Must learn to maintain my distance

It's a question of resistance

I know I shouldn't go

But I can't stay away

Like the rest of them

I'm wasting away

I'm intrigued by vanity, the concept not the act

Observing heartless lack of humanity, separating fiction from fact

Learn to judge them the way they judge themselves

Feel their darkness, enter their personal hell

Lips move as if they believe

That their nonsense is true

No personal identity

The words of others they use

Cannot speak, my words invalid

Unless in agreement, not to be tolerated

Failed the game, failed in life

False sense of security in the shine of the knife

The final step, the greatest leap

The closer I get the more I weep

For false security forgotten in maturity

Eternal child stunted through fear

Clouds in my Eyes

When the sun turns black

And fog covers the eyes

Darkness eases through

A once pure sight, demonic

Trends now come to light

The clouds my eyes

Fog up the skies

Skewer my vision,

Play with my mind

The clouds in my eyes

They carry my fears

Growing darker and darker

Till they spill my tears

She sits alone in the dark

Scrolls down thoughts of corruption

And calls this art

Blue veins tempting the knife

How can death be more painful than life?

Today was a good day

A smile, it lingered on her face

What was once sanity now

Replaced by blissful delusions

As long as they stay, there

Will be more good days

Honey

Honey, honey,

Sticky sweet

Darlin' you're the death of me

Can't you see what has begun?

All my work has come undone

Far too proud

Far too high

In thine ivory tower in the sky

If there was a chance I could change the past

Can't say I would, that's a laugh

Smoke and mirrors

Broken glass

Some memories weren't meant to last

Just relax and let it go

It can't hurt you if you don't know

Honey, honey

Close your eyes

Time to go to bed

My sweet

Meek Delusion

To those who worship nature

And those praising God

Be careful where you place your faith

Before following a fraud

Careful basing action

On what you believe to be true

For the contents of the mind

Can be rewritten

And they will be

'Tis easier to wallow in a pool of self-indulgence,

To blame the heavens and your fellow man

For your failure to reap what is rightfully yours

Than to pick yourself up

To ask for what you want

And risk rejection

'Tis better to retreat inside

The darkest recesses of your mind

Snuff out traces of the light

Of knowledge, common sense

Of happiness

Better to play the righteous fool

Squander old alliances and make some new

But how long

How long can the delusion

Carry on?

Be careful don't get lost

Sin is easy

Not worth the cost

Pride is most irresistible of all

Once you give in

Then starts the fall...

From desperation to arrogance birth

Though they say it is the meek

Who shall inherit the Earth

Everlasting Winter

I used to have a gentle soul

Then I relinquished all control

One day I'll get back to the start

And mend my fractured heart

Everlasting winter, ever present hail

My stone cold heart as tough as nails

The ice glistens, still no one listens

Independent and removed

I've dug my own tomb

Fear of passion, of fire

Can't deal with the warmth

An icy shield,

Protects from the torch

But frost bite sets in

The numbness begins

Is this really the end?

Maybe all I needed was a friend

Gullible

Hmmm,

Am I certain of what I've seen?

Or has it all been but a dream

I am so gullible

I believe my own lies

Isn't it perfect?

An inconspicuous crime

The face of an angel

My hands are chained

Truth exclusively passes these lips

But thousands exist

A shift in perspective

A memory lost

I can't afford to be introspective

Tenuous sanity the cost

Blissful delusions

Unhinged, deranged

Guess they were right

When they called me strange

The Artist

The artist is a voyeur

Lusting for creation and replication

A thief with no choice

A mute yearning for a voice

The artist sleeps with her eyes open

Grasping for a moment

Time flies on a standstill

But there is beauty in the broken

Mirror, Mirror

Mirror, mirror

Make believe

Show me what I want to see

Mirror, mirror

Looking glass

Help me hide my crooked past

With rosy cheeks

And luscious lash

For most people feel

With their eyes

With a smirk

Crass and careless

No depth beneath the flesh

Mirror, mirror

Looking glass

Alas, I find myself envious

Of the creature looking back

Song of Sorrow

There's always a rainbow after it rains

And wisdom comes from pain

For every death there is a birth

Suffering is not a curse

I'll sing a song of sorrow

That nobody wants to hear

'Tis fine, I understand why

Nobody ever wants to cry

But I'll sing my song of sorrow

To drown my tears

To quench my fears

Scare the monsters under bed

And the demons in my head

Oh I'll write my song of sorrows

And send it away

I'll never sing it again

At least not today

Awakening

Shadows

Most people praise the light

But I think shadows

Are just as nice

The greatest star

Wouldn't shine so bright

If it weren't for the darkest night

Nothing More Dangerous

If you want to hurt others

If you must seek revenge

Take heed at once

There's always time to repent

If you can't forgive

If you can't forget

You're just looking through a cracked lens

And a light hasn't shone yet

Once your iron-grip can grab hold of some patience

The happenings of yesterday near evanescence

Don't blame me

I'm not your mirror

You are what you see

Couldn't be any clearer

Within the wrath and anguish you beset

It's no wonder the calm hasn't broken the storm yet

You want to be strong so you don't have to think

But there's nothing more dangerous

Than strength without wit

It's an insidious road

You dare to tread

Step away from your heart

And look to your head

You want to be strong so you don't have to think

But there's nothing more dangerous

Than strength without wit

Gargoyles and Angel Wings

It's not because of a broken heart

Or defamation to my name

It's not about falling apart

Or playing a game

It's about making it by

One day at a time

I can choose whether to laugh

And whether to cry

So I'll choose clear blue skies

The moon and stars

I'll replace gargoyles with angel wings

No dream too far

In a manner of speaking

There's no lack of control

It's a matter of perspective

You choose your role

Wanton

Fickle as the wind

Wanton as the night begets the dawn

If life is but a jape,

I'll merrily sing its song

Fickle as the seasons pass

As Paradise cries for tides run dry

Desire and disorder's untimely dance

Wanton and craven, I pray

For what once was a wasteland, now a haven

Simple as the truth

Sweet and serendipitous

Meant to sooth

I've been blasphemous then pious too

And now owe this insight, to whom?

My heart has opened

Fickle as the wind

Wanton as the night begets the dawn

I knew at once as I surrendered

The fruit of the garden was mine all along

Not Alone

You say I must be lonely

Walking the streets myself only

And I appreciate the sentiment

I appreciate the concern

And soon to all the merriment

Perhaps I will return

For I am not alone

And I am not lonely

Any more than the stars need the sun

To shine their light boldly

I am not alone

And I am not lonely

I can make my own way

Share my own testimony

The clock is ticking

Time is the key

A collection of moments

Saved only by memory

Free yourself from worry

There is no need

For I am not alone

And I am not lonely

For I've got the entirety

Of the universe inside me

And I'll never be alone

Not remotely

The Mermaid

My tongue is sharp and salty

My head is going soft

I dreamt of radical fountains

But lost my soul to sloth

I've been plucked root and stem

Got phantom pain but can't remember from when

Maybe I'll reclaim my legs

And learn to walk again

Oh, I've been passing time

Floating lame and adrift

Searching for an anchor

Put the brakes on any chances I might miss

If only I'd been stronger

Took the reins when fortune sung

Then I'd have a whole lot of nothing

And something to do all day long

It ain't so bad being lost at sea

I'm doing no harm, no harm done unto me

Went searching for thunder

'Til I was swept into the breeze

Oh, it's the mermaid in me

I never feel found 'til I'm lost at sea

Insomniac

A time for dead to have their dynasty

Now the night has enslaved me

Anxiously awaiting the break of dawn

The sun comes up but my mind is gone

My body moves with the tides

The moon is my only guide

Psychosis and restlessness go hand in hand

This is my curse, no room for reprimand

Body steadfast on the earth

Intellect ponders on life's worth

My soul yearns to roam the heavenly plane

I try not to stray but my resolve wanes

I'd like to get off this runaway train

Carrying all the thoughts I wish would stray

Endless fairy tales, lies told just right

This is an insomniac's birthright

Permanence

Deeper and deeper inside

Deep to the divine

You're experiencing melancholy

Because of the transitory

Nature of the cosmos

Don't hold on to preconceptions

Let go of your misdirection

The ephemeral can't be steadfast

It'll be gone in a second glance

Change as a promise is imminent,

Yet, the present is no less brilliant

Mirror

It's fine if you must hurt me

I really don't mind

I'm just a mirror

And you're a flicker of light

Relinquish your anger

I can stomach the blame

Take heed, dear one

To the mirror reframed

I couldn't help it

And I shouldn't care

Maybe the way you've been treated

Has been unfair

But I'm not really here

I'm just a ghost

What is reflected back to you

Is what you require most

And you'll look right through me

In my place a mirage

What you are really witnessing

Is who you really are

Literacy

I lack the efficacy

And literally the literacy

To extravagantly execute

In an utmost astute

Essentially accurate

Display of feeling

Of innermost reeling

Oh heavens!

In dreams,

I hear the music

Taste the verses

But die they must

Before coming to be

And bereft am I of words on my tongue...

Please

Please,

I just need to be held

For deep in the hollows

Nothing can be felt

The bite of the dark

And the kiss of the wind

My vision closes to the world

And a story begins

As the wolf cries

In the light of the moon

Chaos awakens

And opens her tomb

The stars, her child

By her mischief they smile

Propriety be damned

Let my hair down for a while

At my heels the stones of the cave

And the rocks in my brain

Chaos my sanctuary

If only I could refrain

Please,

I couldn't resist

If you leave now you will be missed

Please,

Take my hand and hold me down

I've trouble keeping myself on the ground

Please,

I've got to get away

From both the future and yesterday

I understand your dissent

But *please*,

Help me find my way back to the present

Lost

A little bit lost

A little bit scared

I'm entirely unprepared

For this thing called maturity

Oh! The absurdity!

Must I conform to conformity?

This worldwide sorority,

I want no part in

I'm losing my patience

I'm damned ungracious

I'll give you money

And you'll give me tears

A little bit lost

A little bit scared

I'll never surrender

Just pave my own roads

The Warrior

The sharpest steel

The softest heart

What has oft been disregarded-

What has oft been torn apart?

In the midst of battle

In the midst of sin

I'll do as I've been told

A matter of strength over wit

But what a conundrum

But what a surprise

Reflected back to me was desolation

When I looked into your eyes

A hint of hesitation

A form a debate

To take a another direction

It is never too late

A masquerade of valiance and reliability

A puppeteer's delight

Doubts breed a dangerous docility

Accepting violence as right

Built a mask of credibility

A cowardly farce

Once I realized my greatest strength

Lied within my vulnerability

The highest victory

And the sweetest defeat

Lies not within the ecstasy of conquer

But with surrender and peace

Unyielding Silence

A barren wasteland

A misty vision

Dreams of serendipity

Awash with derision

Once was I to believe

I thrived on chaos

I thrived on pain

Thought I was being productive

I was naught but a pawn in the game

Once laughter dies

And tears been wept and dried

Left is a hollow, unyielding silence

Could it be?

A sanctuary from the violence

Overtaken my mind

But if strength receives me

And my fears were to leave me

I'll surrender to curiosity

The hollow, unyielding abyss

Surrender to silence

My highest guidance

The cessation

Wasn't a predecessor

Of unyielding desolation

A glorified isolation

Nay,

It was an invitation

A sure fire initiation

To serenity and extinction

Abolishment of restriction

In lieu of emptiness inside me

I was a vessel of receptivity

So be it in absence

Of the ubiquitous word

It is within the silence

That the truth is heard

Time

Ne'er to feel

The hands of time

To grasp a moment

Then let it fly

Who can say what we receive?

Fragments of mirror reframed-

A flickering dance of flame-

A river once crossed, ne'er the same...

The flow of the waters

And a trick of the light

The passage of time

Forsaken tonight

Mayhap we're passengers

Mayhap we drive

Mayhap all my dreams and memories

Are one in time

All there is, is *here*

All there is, is *now*

All there is to do, is *be*

At once, and once for eternity

Glass Castle

I lived in a glass castle

On the edge of a dream

And in this ethereal kingdom

I was the queen

I lived in a glass castle

With glass tables and chairs

Because everything was transparent

I was never unaware

I lived in a glass castle

That danced through the clouds

The walls made of whispers

Silence amidst a crowd

I lived in a glass castle

So fragile and pristine

It was a fortress of serenity

But all I wanted was to scream

I lived in a glass castle

Behind a crystalline pane

Civilization beyond reach

Yet there I remained

I lived in a glass castle

With long winding stairs

The towers kept growing

To look back I wouldn't dare

I lived in a glass castle

A gilded cage no more

I broke through the ceiling

And opened a new door

Rebirth

J Remember

I remember dust and cobwebs

Moonlight silhouettes

I remember finding beauty

After the sunset

I remember, but I wish I could forget

Being unable to get out of bed

I remember hiding from the sun

I remember how it feels,

To feel like you're no one

I remember the long winding stairs

And giving up halfway

And I remember thinking

Who really cares anyway?

I remember, I remember

Because how could I forget?

I remember, I remember

The journeys not over yet

I remember the bell jar

And the broken glass

And I remember thinking

My future is not my past

I Forget

I-

Forget

As time flows

As I make the present my home

A sweet release

Of my burdens I'm freed

And yet...

I sit here forlorn

Because-

I...forget

Who I am and who I was

Merge and disengage because

I am not-

Oh! What do I mean?

For who can observe that which is unseen?

I'll reclaim what once was mine

Breathless moments and fragments in time

Only to give it all right back

Because, once again-

I...forget

I take back any scornful deeds

As well as my anguish

At once, reprieved

Though whether or not I am forgiven

What's done is done, I admit submission

Heed now what I beget,

Because, as always-

I... forget

As I gaze into your eyes

Revealing to me, eternal sunrise

Who I am not and who I wish to be

At home in your heart for all eternity

Within the love I now beset

I could never bring myself to forget

Winds of Change

The winds of change

The storm of resentment

The depth of the heart

Too vast for measurement

A heart too full

And hate too deep

Anchor set in the past

The price of departure too steep

Trapped in a web

One's own anger and dread

Hold on tight, escape this maze

Weather the storm,

You shan't squander the last of your days

Alas,

A ship can't sail against the wind!

A change of course, at last, begins

Storm clouds now may reside

And a change of heart taken in stride

Learning to let go, a lesson derived

The winds of change, at last, have arrived!

I Saw the Stars

I saw the stars

When the world was on fire

With the touch of a hand

I escaped from the pyre

I saw the stars

And a glowing silhouette

My reckoning has come to pass

And I'm not dead yet

I saw the stars

As the heavens bled

I relinquish my anguish

For my phantoms have fled

I saw the stars

When I was lost to despair

Whilst their light shone upon me

I knew someone had heard my prayer

I saw the stars

In the black of the night

Ascending from the depths of depravity

My heart is alight

I saw the stars

And they carry me home

As I gaze into their infinity

I know I'm not alone

I saw the stars

And the shadow of the moon

As the wind whispered a promise

My life would begin soon

The End

(Or the beginning)

99538718R00060

Made in the USA
Columbia, SC
11 July 2018